Who Was?

WORKBOOK

GRADE 2
Language/Reading

Based on the #1 *New York Times* Best-Selling Who Was? Series

Reading passages with comprehension, vocabulary, and writing activities, plus puzzles, mazes, and tons of fun!

written by Wiley Blevins and Linda Ross

PENGUIN WORKSHOP
An Imprint of Penguin Random House LLC, New York

Penguin supports copyright. Copyright fuels creativity, encourages diverse voices, promotes free speech, and creates a vibrant culture. Thank you for buying an authorized edition of this book and for complying with copyright laws by not reproducing, scanning, or distributing any part of it in any form without permission. You are supporting writers and allowing Penguin to continue to publish books for every reader.

Cover illustrations by Nancy Harrison
Interior illustrations by Nancy Harrison, Mattia Cerato, Gary LaCoste, Scott MacNeill, and Chris Vallo

Designed by Dinardo Design

Visit us online at www.penguinrandomhouse.com.

ISBN 9780593224533   10 9 8 7 6 5

Who Was?
WORKBOOK

INSTRUCTIONS

Welcome to the wonderful world of Who Was?, full of history and the famous people who made it memorable. This workbook is packed with fascinating fact-filled passages about people you'll want to learn about. It also has fun activities that will help you become a better reader and writer. Here's what you'll find:

Just for Fun! pages contain crossword puzzles, word searches, pages to draw and color, and more!

Read and Annotate pages are loaded with interesting facts about famous people. Mark up the passages as you read to help you better remember the facts. You can circle, underline, draw, and add notes.

Check Comprehension pages show how much you learned. So, show off!

Build Vocabulary pages help you learn and use new words and word parts. You'll want to impress your friends!

Connect Through Writing pages give you space to be creative and connect what you read to your life.

WHAT A MIX-UP!

Look at the picture and read the clue.
Unscramble the name of the famous Who Was? person.

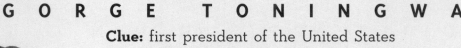

R. D SSSEU

Clue: wrote books like *Green Eggs and Ham*

E GEORGE TONINGWASH

Clue: first president of the United States

K. J. LINGROW

Clue: wrote the Harry Potter books

MCHIELLE OAMAB

Clue: was first lady of the United States

GNIK UTT

Clue: was ruler of ancient Egypt

FAME!

Can you find the **bold-faced** words in the word search below?

F	A	M	O	U	S	F	Q	G	L	E	H
A	U	Z	X	R	E	G	E	N	D	H	I
Y	T	V	S	T	B	C	W	H	L	G	S
Q	H	I	N	V	E	N	T	O	R	M	T
F	O	K	Y	T	H	U	O	N	P	R	O
V	R	S	T	D	I	S	C	O	V	E	R
N	D	I	S	V	R	Z	H	R	N	O	Y
F	H	O	N	R	G	E	N	D	F	V	T
A	X	M	O	L	E	G	E	N	D	U	S
N	D	I	S	V	C	B	V	E	R	L	M

Author: person who writes a book

Discover: to find something new

Famous: well-known

Fan: someone who really likes a well-known person

History: the study of past events

Honor: to remember someone, showing great respect

Inventor: someone who made something new, like a machine

Legend: well-known person who did great things

HIS STORIES WERE FUN!
Dr. Seuss

As you read:

- Underline important words
- Circle confusing words or sentences
- Add drawings or notes to remember important facts

NOTES

_____

_____

_____

_____

_____

_____

_____

_____

_____

_____

"How hard could it be?" some people said, to come up with rhymes from the top of your head! Ted knew it was hard (Dr. Seuss, as he's known) to create books that tickle your funny bone! He taught kids to read in a way that's not done. He taught kids to read in a way that was fun!

Why did Dr. Seuss write *The Cat in the Hat*? He wanted to make learning fun. Lots of teachers did not like it. They thought it was silly. But kids loved *The Cat in the Hat*! Dr. Seuss used peppy rhymes and wild creatures. Learning to read was never the same. Dr. Seuss became a famous author, too.

Dr. Seuss's stories were fun. But they also had serious ideas. *The Sneetches and Other Stories* had a big message. It showed that it is silly for people to hate others who look different. Of all his books, Dr. Seuss liked *The Lorax* the best. It taught how important it is to care for nature. Dr. Seuss loved writing books for children. For him, nothing was more important than that.

What books do you have?
Go ahead, take a look.
Do you have a favorite Dr. Seuss book?

ALL ABOUT WORDS

Complete the word box. For **Drawing**, draw a picture of someone creating something. For **Examples**, write examples of things that have been created, or made. For **Nonexamples**, write examples of things that haven't been created—things that occur naturally.

CREATE

Definition in your own words	**Drawing**
Examples	**Nonexamples**

Synonym (word with the same meaning) _____

Antonym (word with the opposite meaning) _____

Related Words: Complete the word part to make a word with "create."

_____ tive   _____ ing   _____ tion

DR. SEUSS RETELLING PYRAMID

_____

What job did Dr. Seuss have?

_____ _____

What was Dr. Seuss's favorite book?

_____ _____ _____

In three words, describe Dr. Seuss's books.

_____

Besides his favorite, name another famous Dr. Seuss book.

What's the most interesting thing you learned about Dr. Seuss?

_____

_____

What else would you like to learn about Dr. Seuss?

_____

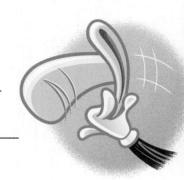

_____

SCARY STORIES
Maurice Sendak

NOTES

_____
_____
_____
_____
_____
_____
_____
_____
_____
_____

Maurice Sendak loved scary stories! His father liked to tell him stories from Poland. That was where his father was born. He told Maurice stories about scary ghosts. There were also tales about children who got lost in the forest. Maurice got in trouble when he told these stories at school.

Maurice grew up to be an author of children's books. He won lots of awards. His most famous book was _Where the Wild Things Are_. It was published in 1963. Back then, most children's books showed the world as a safe place. But not Maurice's books! He wanted to be different.

The "Wild Things" in Maurice's book are monsters with sharp teeth. They say they will eat Max, the hero of the story. To Maurice, they were a lot like his family from Poland. They were big and loud. They would pinch his cheeks. They would say, "You're so cute! I could eat you up."

People worried that the book might scare children. But Maurice knew it was okay for kids to read about his "Wild Things." Even as a child, he knew that the world was full of monsters. The best way to deal with them was to do what Max did. You stare them in the eyes! You show them who's boss!

TRUE OR FALSE?

Read each sentence about Maurice Sendak. Write **true** or **false** on the line. Then write another true sentence about Maurice Sendak on the last lines.

_____ **1.** Maurice's father used to tell him scary stories.

_____ **2.** Maurice's father was born in Italy.

_____ **3.** Maurice didn't like scary stories.

_____ **4.** *Where the Wild Things Are* was Maurice's most famous book.

_____ **5.** The "Wild Things" in Maurice's book were robots from outer space.

_____ **6.** Some people worried that Maurice's book was too scary for children.

7. _____

_____

_____

FAMILY PORTRAIT

Pick a family member. Write a favorite memory.

_____

(title)

_____

_____

_____

_____

_____

_____

_____

Write three words to describe this person.

_____   _____   _____

A DARK AND SILENT WORLD
Helen Keller

As you read:
- Underline important words
- Circle confusing words or sentences
- Add drawings or notes to remember important facts

NOTES

_____
_____
_____
_____
_____
_____
_____
_____
_____
_____

Helen Keller was born more than 100 years ago. When a bad sickness left her both deaf and blind as a toddler, she eventually learned to speak, read, and write after years of hard work with a patient teacher.

Imagine that your ears are stuffed with cotton. You can't hear anything. A blindfold covers your eyes. You can't see anything, either. As a young girl, Helen's world was dark and silent. She felt lonely and frustrated because she wanted to communicate better with the people around her, but she didn't yet have a way to do that.

When Helen was growing up, few deaf people learned how to speak. And few blind people learned to read and write. This was because there were very few schools for deaf and blind people. But Helen wanted to feel better and her parents were able to find her a devoted teacher who helped her develop the tools she would need to accomplish her goals. She ended up writing several best-selling books. She gave lectures around the world. And above all, she gave hope to other people like her about what was possible if given access to education.

PREFIX CONNECT

Helen Keller was one of the most famous people with **disabilities** in history. But she was **able** to read, write, and do so much more. The prefix **dis-** means "not" or the "opposite of." Draw a line to connect a prefix and a word to make a new word. Then write the new word above its definition.

dis = not or opposite of
re = again or back
mis = wrong, bad, or opposite

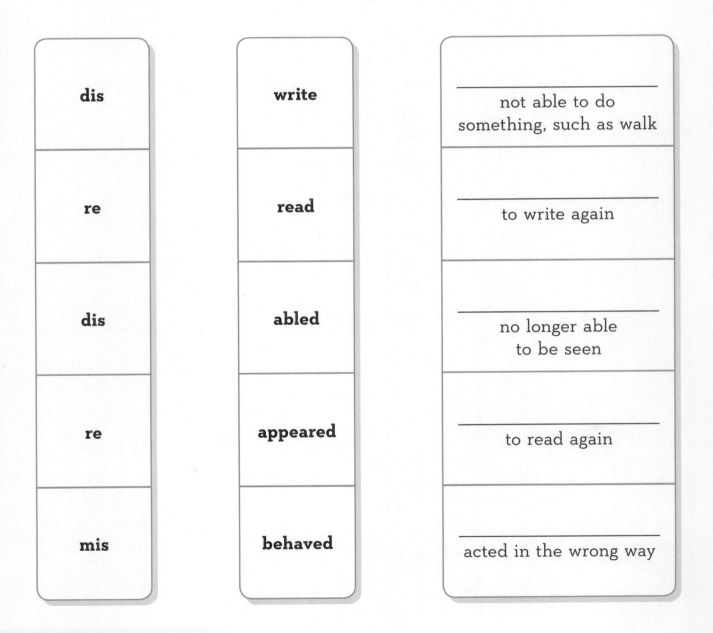

dis	write	_____ not able to do something, such as walk
re	read	_____ to write again
dis	abled	_____ no longer able to be seen
re	appeared	_____ to read again
mis	behaved	_____ acted in the wrong way

HAIKU

Haiku is a kind of poem. It has three lines. Each line has a specific number of syllables. Write a haiku describing Helen Keller.

Helen Keller

(5 syllables) _____

(7 syllables) _____

(5 syllables) _____

Now write a haiku describing you.

Me

(5 syllables) _____

(7 syllables) _____

(5 syllables) _____

FAMOUS JOBS

Answer the clues to test what you know
about these famous peoples' jobs.

CLUES

ACROSS

2. works to change things to help those who
are treated badly

5. works for the government

7. writes books, stories, poems, and plays

DOWN

1. paints pictures

3. invents, or makes, new things

4. plays sports

6. appears in movies or plays

Laura Ingalls
Wilder

Pablo Picasso

Steve Jobs

Charlie Chaplin

CROSSWORD

George Washington

Answer Choices

actor	politician
writer	athlete
inventor	painter
activist	

Jesse Owens

Jane Goodall

MEETING THE KING

King Tut

As you read:
- Underline important words
- Circle confusing words or sentences
- Add drawings or notes to remember important facts

NOTES

_____

_____

_____

_____

_____

_____

_____

_____

_____

_____

_____

King Tut was a pharaoh, or king, of Egypt. He died long ago. He was buried in a secret tomb. King Tut was lucky. Until Howard Carter found his burial chamber, his mummy had never been disturbed, and no one had tried to rob his tomb for more than 3,000 years.

In the burial chamber, the first thing Carter saw was a giant gold cabinet. Inside that was a great stone box. And inside that was the outer mummy case. It was solid gold.

When Carter raised its lid, there it was— under a mask of gold, the cloth-covered mummy of Tut. Then he carefully peeled away strips of cloth. He was face-to-face with Tut. The pharaoh's face looked young and peaceful.

Nearby was a chest made of white stone, called alabaster. Inside were jars holding Tut's organs. The priests had removed them from his body so long ago.

The treasures of Tut's tomb were sent to a museum in Cairo, Egypt. But Howard Carter did not send the king's mummy there. It stayed in the tomb, right where it belonged. That is where it remains now—in peace.

HIEROGLYPHS

The ancient Egyptians used symbols, called hieroglyphs, to write. Look at the hieroglyph key. Use it to write the words. Then draw a line from the word to its meaning.

A	B	C or K	D	E or I	F or V	G
H	J	L	M	N	O	P
Q	R	S	T	U or W	Y	Z

Hieroglyph	Write Word	Meaning
	_____	king or ruler
	_____	a metal
	_____	a body preserved after death
	_____	place where art and artifacts are kept
	_____	place someone is buried

KING TUT RETELLING PYRAMID

_____

Where did Tut live?

_____ _____

Who found Tut's tomb?

_____ _____ _____

Name three things found in Tut's tomb.

_____

Write a sentence about Tut.

What's the most interesting thing you learned about King Tut?

_____

_____

What else would you like to learn about King Tut?

_____

_____

YOU ARE SPECIAL
Mister Rogers

NOTES

_____

_____

_____

_____

_____

_____

_____

_____

_____

_____

"Hi, neighbor." In 1966, Fred Rogers made a TV show for children. It was called *Mister Rogers' Neighborhood*. Fred Rogers starred in it.

Growing up, Fred did not always fit in with other kids. He was shy. He got sick a lot, too. But he learned how just one person can change someone's life. That is what he wanted his show to teach. People are special just by being who they are. Fred hoped to help kids see that.

On his show, Mister Rogers took kids to great places. They went to a crayon factory. They visited a mushroom farm. They also went to The Neighborhood of Make-Believe. It was a royal kingdom where puppets lived.

Fred knew kids had lots of questions. Did getting a haircut hurt? How did people get in and out of the TV? Fred tried to answer them all. Talking about things made people feel better. Nothing was too small for him to talk about. Nothing was too big.

Fred earned many honors for helping children. He got the Presidential Medal of Freedom. There is a Mister Rogers postage stamp. There is even an asteroid named after him!

NOTES

SYNONYM BUCKETS

Synonyms are words that mean the same or nearly the same. Choose words from the word bank to fill the synonym buckets. Add other words you know.

Word Bank

bashful	**wonderful**	**speaking**	**area**
terrific	**timid**	**community**	**chatting**

neighborhood

_____

_____

_____

shy

_____

_____

_____

great

_____

_____

_____

talking

_____

_____

_____

LETTER TIME

Kids wrote letters to Mister Rogers all the time. Write a letter to someone you know telling them about Mister Rogers.

Dear _____ ,

_____

_____

_____

_____

_____

_____

Your friend,

_____

REACH FOR THE STARS
Sally Ride

As you read:

- Underline important words
- Circle confusing words or sentences
- Add drawings or notes to remember important facts

NOTES

_____

_____

_____

_____

_____

_____

_____

_____

_____

_____

Lift off! Sally Ride was the first American woman in space!

In 1977, the U.S. space program was looking for new astronauts. The right person had to be smart. He or she had to be a team player, too. Thousands of people applied. But there were only 35 spots. Sally Ride got the job!

The training was hard. It took many years. At last, on June 18, 1983, Sally was going into outer space! She would be inside the space shuttle for six days. She would be 200 miles from Earth.

When the shuttle reached outer space, the force of gravity was gone. Sally thought being weightless was fun. The astronauts watched their pencils and books float by. They even did flips in the air.

The astronauts did important work in space. They took lots of pictures. They also did many experiments. The mission was very successful!

When Sally was older, she gave speeches to young students. She wanted them to seek careers in science. She especially wanted to inspire girls. How did Sally end every talk? She told students to "reach for the stars!"

NOTES

BLAST OFF!

Write four facts you learned about Sally Ride.

1. _____

   _____

   _____

   _____

2. _____

   _____

   _____

   _____

3. _____

   _____

   _____

   _____

4. _____

   _____

   _____

ALL ABOUT THE ENDING

A suffix is a word part added to the end of a word. It changes the word's meaning. Finish each sentence using a word from the word bank. Use each word's suffix as a clue.

Word Bank			
player	successful	weightless	outer

1. You float in space because you are _____ .

2. Sally Ride was happy that her mission was _____ .

3. Sally traveled 200 miles from Earth into _____ space.

4. An astronaut has to be a good team _____ .

CONNECT THE DOTS

Thomas Alva Edison was an inventor. He invented many things, such as the motion picture camera and the first long-lasting electric _____ . Connect the dots to see the invention, and then finish the sentence with that word.

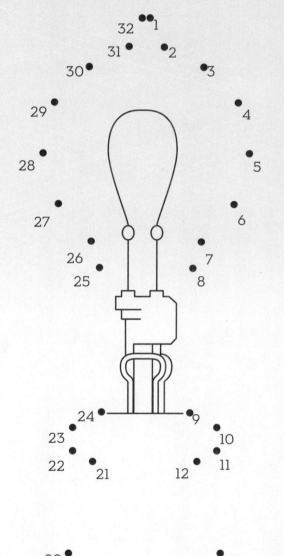

THE AMAZING FRANKLIN MAZE

Benjamin Franklin lived in the 1700s. He did many important things. He was a writer, scientist, inventor, politician, postmaster, and more. He was also very funny! Help Ben find his way to Independence Hall.

APPLES, APPLES, AND MORE APPLES
Johnny Appleseed

As you read:

- Underline important words
- Circle confusing words or sentences
- Add drawings or notes to remember important facts

NOTES

_____

_____

_____

_____

_____

_____

_____

_____

_____

Johnny Appleseed's real name was John Chapman. He got his nickname by planting apple seeds across America.

Johnny lived in Massachusetts during Colonial times. America was growing at that time. Johnny saw settlers moving west. So he went west, too. He wanted to grow apple trees. The settlers would need fruit on their land.

Johnny didn't bring much on his travels. He didn't even wear shoes! He liked to be different. He never settled in one place. He enjoyed living alone in the beautiful wilderness. But it wasn't easy! He sometimes slept in hollow trees. One winter, he only had nuts to eat.

Johnny always knew where people would move next. He would get there first and plant apple trees. He brought apple seedlings and news from other places. He told people stories about his adventures, too.

People started to tell tall tales about Johnny. He became very famous. Stories about him spread from town to town. And they got taller every time! Johnny didn't leave a diary or any letters to tell about his life. But luckily, his tall tales tell it all!

SYLLABLE SORT

Words have syllables. Each syllable has one vowel sound. Chunking long words by syllable can help you read them. Find the first syllable in each word in the word bank. Write it in the correct column.

Word Bank

people	winter	famous	settlers
even	diary	planting	Chapman

Open Syllable
ends in a vowel and has a long vowel sound

_____

_____

_____

_____

Closed Syllable
ends in a consonant and has a short vowel sound

_____

_____

_____

_____

Write the meanings of the words below. Use clues from the story.

settlers: _____

nickname: _____

DESCRIPTION SUMMARY FRAME

Johnny Appleseed lived during Colonial times. He _____

_____

_____ .

Johnny was a different sort of fellow. People thought it was strange

that he _____

_____

_____ .

When Johnny traveled from place to place, he brought _____

_____

_____ .

Apples were a popular food of the settlers.

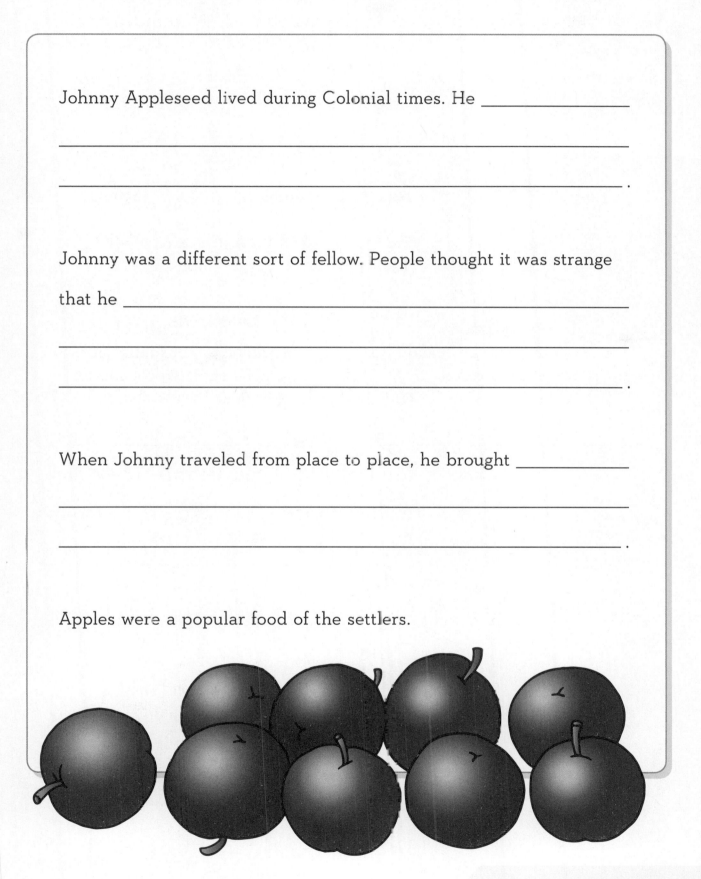

THE KEY TO SUCCESS
H. J. Heinz

As you read:

- Underline important words
- Circle confusing words or sentences
- Add drawings or notes to remember important facts

NOTES

_____

_____

_____

_____

_____

_____

_____

_____

_____

_____

Henry John Heinz sold the freshest products and the best-tasting. He wanted his customers to know one thing—any food he delivered was worth the money they spent! And people grew to trust the Heinz name. Henry built one of the largest food companies in the world. He moved his growing company to Pittsburgh, Pennsylvania. There, he built factories. He used the most modern

ways to process and package food. He also thought up new ways to attract customers. One way was to come up with a slogan. That's a phrase describing a company and its products. Henry's slogan was "57 Varieties." He put it on all his labels. Now, everyone knew he sold many products, from pickles to baked beans.

Selling food might seem easy. Everyone has to eat. And many people don't have time to grow crops or prepare their own foods. So, Henry made better-quality food. He sold more than anyone else. His hard work and smart ideas proved one of his favorite sayings. "To do a common thing uncommonly well brings success."

NOTES

_____

_____

_____

_____

_____

_____

_____

_____

_____

_____

_____

WRITE A SLOGAN

A slogan is a phrase describing a company and its products. Draw pictures of things you buy or need, such as food, tennis shoes, or toys. Write the slogan used to sell each one.

57 Varieties

UNCOMMONLY GOOD

What made H. J. Heinz so successful? Write four facts you learned about him.

1. _____

_____

_____

2. _____

_____

_____

3. _____

_____

_____

4. _____

_____

_____

THE SEWING LEGEND
Betsy Ross

As you read:
- Underline important words
- Circle confusing words or sentences
- Add drawings or notes to remember important facts

NOTES

_____
_____
_____
_____
_____
_____
_____
_____
_____
_____

There's a great American legend. It says Betsy Ross sewed the first American flag. Is it true? Her family says so! It's a story that has become a part of the country's early history.

Nearly 100 years after the Revolutionary War, Betsy's family told this story. Three men visited Betsy at her shop in Philadelphia. One was her husband's uncle, George Ross. He was aware of Betsy's sewing skills. The second was Robert Morris. He was very rich. He helped raise money to pay for the war. The third man was George Washington. He would go on to be our first president!

When the three men visited Betsy, they brought a sketch of a flag. They needed to have a sample made. Betsy showed them how to make it better. The men had drawn a square flag. Betsy said it should be longer. The sketch showed 13 red and white stripes. There was one stripe for each of the 13 colonies. A blue square in the upper left corner had 13 stars. Each star had six points. Betsy felt that a star with five points was better. Making stars this way would be faster and easier. But did she really sew that first flag? No one can say for sure.

OUR FIRST FLAG

Color the flag using details from the story.

Write three interesting facts about the flag.

1. _____

_____

2. _____

_____

3. _____

_____

YOU'RE A LEGEND!

Write about someone who is, or could become, a legend because of their great deeds.

COMIC TIME!

Make your own comic strip. Tell the story of someone famous.
Or tell about a big event in your life.

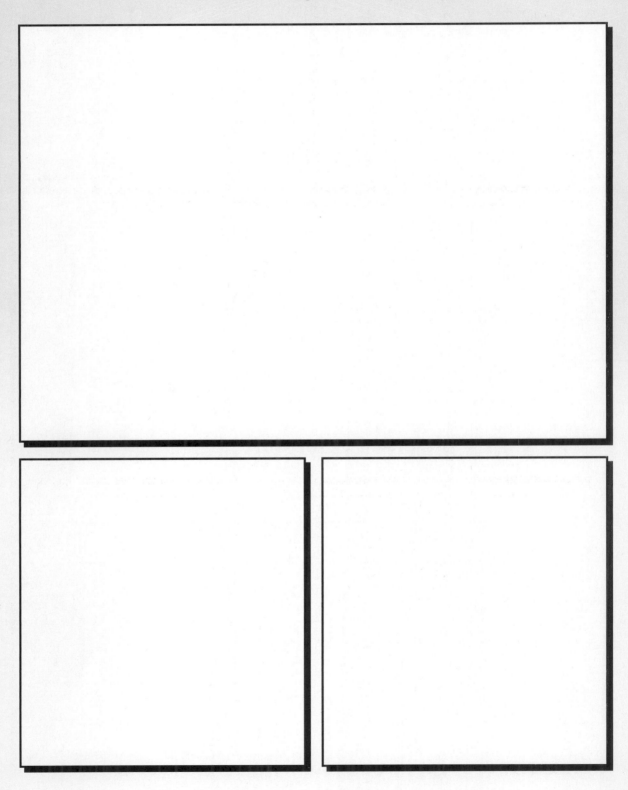

PEANUTS
George Washington Carver

1809

As you read:

- Underline important words
- Circle confusing words or sentences
- Add drawings or notes to remember important facts

NOTES

_____

_____

_____

_____

_____

_____

_____

_____

_____

George Washington Carver was a scientist and an inventor. He developed products made from peanuts, like plastics, soaps, and dyes.

Long ago, peanuts were mostly used to feed animals. Farmers couldn't make much money growing them. So, they had little reason to do so. But George changed that! Farmers liked to grow cotton. But the cotton plants took too many nutrients out of the soil. So, they needed to plant something else every other year that would add nutrients to the soil.

George suggested more farmers grow peanuts.

In 1916, George wrote a famous booklet about peanuts. It had recipes in it. Peanut soup. Peanut bread. Peanut pudding. Yum! Several recipes used peanut butter. That same year, George got a big honor. It was from the Royal Society of Arts in London. It honored people who find everyday solutions to problems. That's what George did. At the time, it was rare for an American to get this honor. It was especially important because George was born into slavery. An enslaved person is a person who is owned by another person. They are forced to work for the owners and do whatever the owners tell them to do. But George rose above his hard, early years. Now he was changing the world!

PROBLEM/SOLUTION SUMMARY FRAME

George Washington Carver was a scientist and an inventor. He spent his life solving problems.

One problem he solved had to do with the use of peanuts. Peanuts were a problem because _____

_____.

Carver solved this problem by _____

_____

and _____

_____.

Now we use peanuts for many things. Farmers make a lot of money growing them, too.

YUM! IT'S RECIPE TIME!

What food do you like made from peanuts? Fill in the recipe card for this food. Or make up your own recipe!

Recipe

Peanut _____

Ingredients:

1. _____

_____

2. _____

_____

3. _____

_____

4. _____

_____

LET'S DANCE!
Maria Tallchief

NOTES

_____
_____
_____
_____
_____
_____
_____
_____
_____
_____

Maria Tallchief was a ballerina. America's first prima ballerina. A prima ballerina is the star of the show. She is the best dancer on the stage. Maria danced for many people, including kings, queens, and presidents. She thrilled her audiences with amazing leaps. She performed as a swan queen, a sugar plum fairy, and a magical firebird. Her performances were some of the most beautiful in America.

Maria was Native American. She lived on the Osage reservation in the rolling hills of Oklahoma. A reservation is land set aside for Native Americans by the U.S. government. As a child, the beat of the tom-toms excited her. The

rhythm of the drums filled the hollow
of her bones. The songs of her people's
past woke within her a love of dance.
That led to her becoming a professional
dancer. Maria performed until she was
41. After that, she retired. But she never
stopped dancing. She made a studio on
the top floor of her house. Each day,
she put her ballet shoes to work! Maria
died at the age of 88. People around
the world remember her as one of the
greatest ballerinas.

BROTHER AND SISTER WORDS

Some words are related, like brothers and sisters. They come from the same base word. Look at the words in the word bank. Use them to fill in the chart.

Word Bank			
perform	**magic**	**excite**	**dance**
performer	**magical**	**excited**	**dancer**
performance	**magician**	**excitement**	**dancing**

NOUN names a person, place, or thing	**VERB** action word	**ADJECTIVE** describing word
_____	_____	_____
_____	_____	_____
_____	_____	_____
_____	_____	_____
_____	_____	_____

ALL ABOUT MARIA

Fill in each blank to show what you learned about Maria Tallchief.

1. Maria was a _____ woman

   and a daughter of Osage parents.

2. Maria was one of the best ballerinas in the U.S.

   She was a _____ ballerina.

3. Maria _____ for everyone—

   from kings and queens to her family and friends.

4. Maria stopped dancing as a job when she

   _____ at age 41.

Draw Maria performing.

SOCCER TIME

Pelé

As you read:

- Underline important words
- Circle confusing words or sentences
- Add drawings or notes to remember important facts

NOTES

_____

_____

_____

_____

_____

_____

_____

_____

Pelé is a retired star soccer player. He became the most famous player in the world. He had money, and he had success. But it didn't start out that way. Pelé grew up in Brazil. He was born Edson Arantes do Nascimento. Every boy in his neighborhood played soccer. He spent hours playing with them. He was fast. Even though he was small for his age, he was one of the best.

The boys were too poor to buy a ball. So, they got an old sock. They stuffed it with rags. Then, they tied it up with string. This became their soccer ball. The goalposts were an old pair of shoes. There were no real fields and few organized leagues for kids.

Edson did have one advantage—his father. He was a great player who liked showing the boys all that he knew about the game he loved. He told them about the positions on the field. A forward's main job is to score goals. And the goalkeeper's job is to stop them!

They practiced dribbling and passing the soccer ball. He taught them how to shoot the ball at the goal and how to control the ball. Edson loved this time with his father. "One day," he told his friends, "I'm going to be as good as my dad." He became even better!

ALL ABOUT WORDS

Look at the word in each soccer ball. Write a fact from the story using each word.

poor

_____

_____

_____

advantage

_____

_____

_____

league

_____

_____

_____

positions

_____

_____

_____

GAME TIME!

Write about a game or sport you know how to play.

Keys to Playing _____

1. _____

2. _____

3. _____

4. _____

Picture of Kids Playing _____

Why I Recommend It

_____

_____

_____

_____

SEARCH FOR IT!

Read the facts about some well-known people.
Find the **bold-faced** words in the word search.

C	M	A	G	I	C	I	A	N	L	D	Y
M	O	V	S	C	O	O	D	X	B	L	V
R	V	P	A	D	O	X	T	O	N	S	M
U	I	T	V	Y	K	D	L	C	S	I	U
A	E	X	P	E	D	I	T	I	O	N	I
M	S	A	T	E	C	H	O	D	L	G	N
U	M	L	E	D	Y	T	R	W	Q	E	P
S	Z	X	S	L	A	D	Y	U	I	R	F
I	J	M	S	H	C	O	L	O	P	T	U
C	H	O	C	O	L	A	T	E	R	R	M

Dolly Parton is a famous **singer**.

Julia Child taught people how to **cook**.

Harry Houdini was a master **magician**.

Bruce Lee was a martial artist who made **movies**.

Elvis Presley was known as "The King of Rock 'n' Roll" **music**.

Milton Hershey was a candymaker, famous for his **chocolate**.

Eleanor Roosevelt was once the first **lady** of the U.S.

Sacagawea helped Lewis and Clark on their **expedition**.

WHAT A MIX-UP!

Look at the picture and read the clue.
Unscramble the name of the famous Who Was? person.

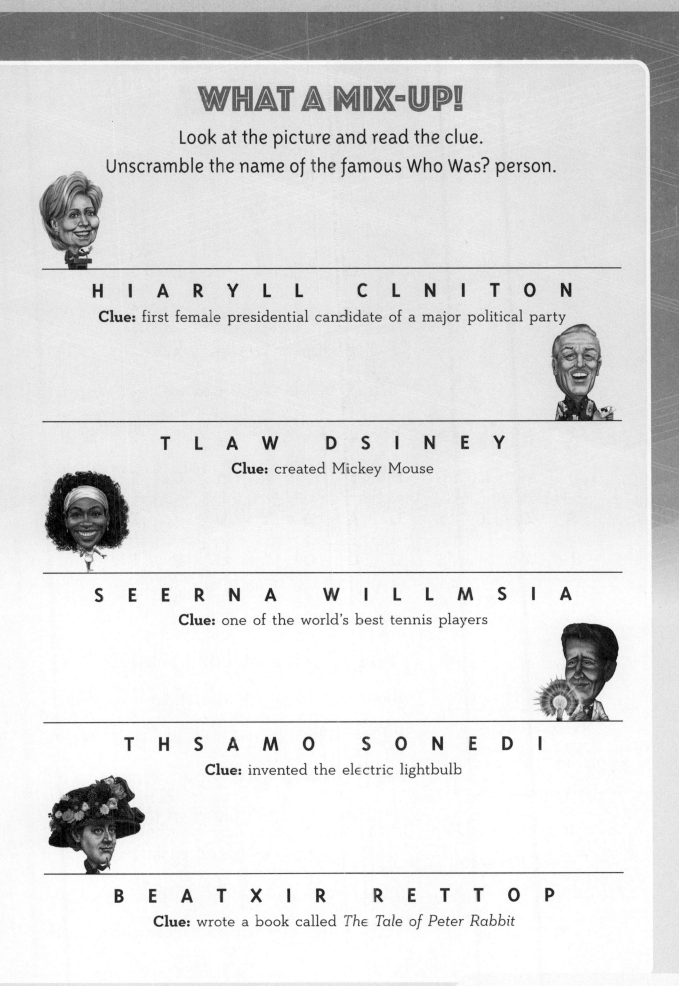

H I A R Y L L   C L N I T O N

Clue: first female presidential candidate of a major political party

T L A W   D S I N E Y

Clue: created Mickey Mouse

S E E R N A   W I L L M S I A

Clue: one of the world's best tennis players

T H S A M O   S O N E D I

Clue: invented the electric lightbulb

B E A T X I R   R E T T O P

Clue: wrote a book called *The Tale of Peter Rabbit*

SEEING A SOLUTION
Louis Braille

As you read:

- Underline important words
- Circle confusing words or sentences
- Add drawings or notes to remember important facts

NOTES

_____
_____
_____
_____
_____
_____
_____
_____
_____
_____

Louis Braille grew up in a small town in France. When he was three years old, he had a terrible accident. It left him blind. But being blind did not stop him. Living in the dark made him even more curious about the world. Louis couldn't read or write. But he could listen and remember. He was one of the best students at his school.

When he was 10, Louis went to Paris. He went to study at a school for the blind. The library had 14 books. They were printed with raised, or embossed, letters. Blind people read them with their fingers. It wasn't easy. Each letter was large. You had to trace it with many fingers. Then you had to remember the letter. Since the letters were large, the books had many pages. They weighed as much as nine pounds!

At school, Louis learned about "night writing." Night writing was created to help soldiers read and write in the dark. It used a code of raised dots. It worked better. But it had problems, too.

Louis wanted to invent his own system. By the time he was 15, he figured it out! He found a way for blind people to read and write easily. He even added math and music symbols to his code! Today, people all over the world still use his system. It is called braille.

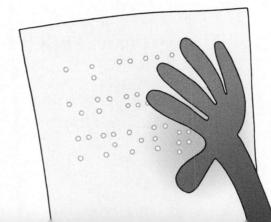

READING BRAILLE

Look at the braille chart. Write words from the story using the chart. Draw a line from the word to its meaning.

A	B	C	D	E	F	G	H	I
J	K	L	M	N	O	P	Q	R
S	T	U	V	W	X	Y	Z	

Braille	Write Word	Meaning
	_____	system of writing using dots
	_____	not able to see
	_____	to make something new
	_____	very bad

SEQUENCE SUMMARY FRAME

When Louis Braille was three years old, _____

_____

_____ .

At age 10, _____

_____

_____ .

There, he _____

_____

_____ .

Finally, at age 15 _____

_____

_____ .

Today, people all over the world still use braille.

FAMILY CAME FIRST
Michelle Obama

As you read:

- Underline important words
- Circle confusing words or sentences
- Add drawings or notes to remember important facts

NOTES

_____
_____
_____
_____
_____
_____
_____
_____
_____

Living in the White House was exciting! But for Michelle Obama, family always came first.

Michelle met Barack Obama when she was a lawyer. Later on, they got married and had a family. Raising kids was not easy for two working parents. But Michelle made things work. Her parents had taught her that respect, love, and hard work were important. She would do the same with her daughters, Malia and Sasha.

In 2008, Barack became president. The U.S. had its first African American president—and first lady! As first lady, Michelle had important jobs to do.

Being a first lady and a mom kept her very busy!

Michelle had rules! No whining, arguing, or teasing. The girls still had chores. There would be no photos of the girls without permission. She wanted to protect them. She also wanted them to have a normal life.

Barack was reelected in 2012. Michelle was happy to go on being the first lady. Barack Obama was the Commander in Chief. But Michelle was the "mom in chief." Being a good parent was her most important job.

ALL ABOUT WORDS

Complete the word box. For **Drawing**, draw a picture that shows someone protecting something. For **Examples**, write examples of things that are protected. For **Nonexamples**, write examples of things that are not protected.

PROTECT	
Definition in your own words	**Drawing**
Examples	**Nonexamples**

Synonym (word with the same meaning) _____

Antonym (word with the opposite meaning) _____

Related Words: Complete the word part to make a word with "protect."

_____ tion _____ ing _____ tive

FASCINATING FACTS

Write four facts you learned from the story about Michelle Obama.

1. _____
   _____
   _____

2. _____
   _____
   _____

3. _____
   _____
   _____

4. _____
   _____
   _____

As you read:

- Underline important words
- Circle confusing words or sentences
- Add drawings or notes to remember important facts

NOTES

_____
_____
_____
_____
_____
_____
_____
_____
_____

Finally! Sonia Sotomayor got the call! The president wanted her to be a judge on the Supreme Court.

Sonia never imagined it could happen. When she was eight, she didn't feel well. She lost energy and weight. Her mom took her to a doctor. They got some bad news. She had type 1 diabetes. People with this disease can't get energy from food. They need injections of a medicine called insulin. Insulin helps keep them healthy.

Sonia's parents were too nervous to give her the insulin shots. But Sonia loved to solve problems. So, she gave herself insulin shots every day!

Sonia thought about her future. She wanted to help people. So she became a lawyer. Lawyers work long hours. Sonia had to be careful. She had to balance her insulin and food. She also had to exercise. She always wanted to be her best.

When President Obama chose her to be a Supreme Court judge, he wanted to be sure that she would stay healthy. He wanted her to work on the court for many years. Sonia didn't let her disease stop her! She became the first Hispanic person to be a Supreme Court justice. Way to go!

SONIA SUMMARY

Write a summary of "Nothing Could Stop Her." Use four sentences. Include only the most important facts.

_____

_____

_____

_____

_____

_____

_____

_____

_____

_____

_____

WHEN I WAS A KID

Sonia's visit to the doctor changed her life. Write about a memory from your life—happy or sad. Why was it an important day or event?

FAMOUS PEOPLE

Answer the clues to test what you know about these famous people.

CLUES

ACROSS

2. Rosa Parks was called the "First Lady of Civil _____."

3. Frida Kahlo was a painter living in _____.

4. Neil Armstrong was the first person to step on the _____.

6. Roberto Clemente was a great _____ player.

DOWN

1. Amelia Earhart flew across the Atlantic _____.

2. Harriet Tubman led enslaved people to freedom on the Underground _____.

5. Anne Frank wrote a famous _____.

Frida
Kahlo

Rosa
Parks

Neil
Armstrong

CROSSWORD

Roberto Clemente

Harriet Tubman

Anne Frank

Amelia Earhart

Answer Choices

diary

Rights

moon

Railroad

baseball

Ocean

Mexico

FAIRY TALE COLLECTORS
The Brothers Grimm

As you read:
- Underline important words
- Circle confusing words or sentences
- Add drawings or notes to remember important facts

NOTES

_____
_____
_____
_____
_____
_____
_____
_____
_____
_____
_____

The Brothers Grimm collected fairy tales. But it was a hard job! Why? Few tales had been written down. People knew a tale because someone had told it to them. So there was just one way to collect the tales. Listen to people who knew them by heart. The brothers traveled to find these people. They listened to them tell their stories. Then, they wrote them down, word for word. They had to make sure these special tales would not be lost!

What is a fairy tale? It is a quest story. That is a story where someone is searching for something. It is often about a hero who overcomes evil. A fairy tale may use magic, too. There are make-believe creatures, like giants and elves. There may also be animals that talk. A fairy tale is set long ago in a faraway place. It often begins with "once upon a time."

No one knows who created fairy tales. And the details in these stories can sometimes change. For example, in Germany, Snow White lived with seven dwarfs. But in Albania, she lived with forty dragons. Thanks to the Brothers Grimm, we still have these tales. We get to read about Cinderella, Little Red Riding Hood, Sleeping Beauty, and many more.

NOTES

_____

_____

_____

_____

_____

_____

_____

_____

_____

_____

_____

_____

WHAT IS A FAIRY TALE?

Use facts from the story. Write what you know about fairy tales.

Characteristics

1. _____

2. _____

3. _____

4. _____

Examples

1. _____

2. _____

3. _____

4. _____

FAIRY TALE RETELLING

Choose your favorite fairy tale. Write a retelling. Or write your own funny version of the tale.

_____

_____

_____

_____

_____

_____

_____

_____

_____

_____

_____

_____

_____

_____

MALALA AND THE UNITED NATIONS
Malala Yousafzai

As you read:
- Underline important words
- Circle confusing words or sentences
- Add drawings or notes to remember important facts

NOTES

_____

_____

_____

_____

_____

_____

_____

_____

_____

_____

When Malala was shot, the news spread quickly. All around the world, people were horrified. This young girl had wanted to go to school. She had written a diary. She had spoken out that all girls should be able to go to school. For this, she nearly lost her life.

A month later, the Secretary-General of the United Nations declared that July 12, 2013, would be Malala Day. It would be her 16th birthday.

Malala was invited to speak at the United Nations Youth Assembly. Every year, young people

from all over the world meet with UN diplomats. Diplomats are people who are sent from their home country to meet with and talk to diplomats from other countries. They try to find solutions to common problems. They talk about what children in their countries go through and what can be done to help improve their lives. Some children are forced to work hard jobs at a young age. Some very young girls are forced to marry. Some, like Malala, are told they can't go to school.

By the summer of 2013, Malala was well enough to travel to the United Nations. She had spent nine months recovering from her injuries. Her operations were successful. Malala was ready to show the world one important thing—that a terrorist with a gun had not stopped her. She would continue to speak out!

NOTES

_____

_____

_____

_____

_____

_____

_____

_____

_____

_____

_____

_____

DEFINE, EXAMPLE, ASK

Look at each word. Write a definition for the word. Use clues from the story. Then write an example sentence using the word. Finally, write a question using the word that you could ask a friend.

horrified	Define: _____ Example: _____ Ask: _____ _____
improve	Define: _____ Example: _____ Ask: _____ _____
declared	Define: _____ Example: _____ Ask: _____ _____
diplomat	Define: _____ Example: _____ Ask: _____ _____

MALALA RETELLING PYRAMID

_____

What is the girl's name?

_____ _____

What organization made July 12, 2013, Malala Day?

_____ _____ _____

In three words, describe Malala.

Finish this sentence: Malala wanted _____

_____ .

What's the most interesting thing you learned about Malala?

_____

_____

What else would you like to learn about Malala?

_____

_____

THE MUPPETS AND MORE
Jim Henson

As you read:
- Underline important words
- Circle confusing words or sentences
- Add drawings or notes to remember important facts

NOTES

Jim Henson was the man behind the Muppets. He was Kermit the Frog. He was Ernie of Sesame Street. But at first, puppets were just a way for him to get on TV. That was what he really wanted to do.

Although he could be shy, he landed a job in TV as a teenager. In college, he got his very own TV puppet show!

Until Jim Henson, hand puppets and marionettes with strings were the most common kinds of puppets. He invented a new kind. Jim's puppets didn't look like most puppets. His were crazy, oddball creatures. He called them Muppets.

Jim was a tall, thin, soft-spoken guy. He looked gentle and serious—not silly. But from the start, his Muppets were wild and goofy. Today, his Big Bird, Miss Piggy, and Kermit the Frog are known around the world. He helped make *Sesame Street* one of the most popular children's shows ever.

Jim wanted to get on TV. And he did. But he also made a difference in the world.

SYNONYM MATCH

Synonyms are words that mean the same or almost the same.
Match the synonyms.

silly
shy
thin
gentle
wild
popular

untamed
timid
funny
well-known
slender
calm

Write a synonym for each word below.

quiet _____   fast _____

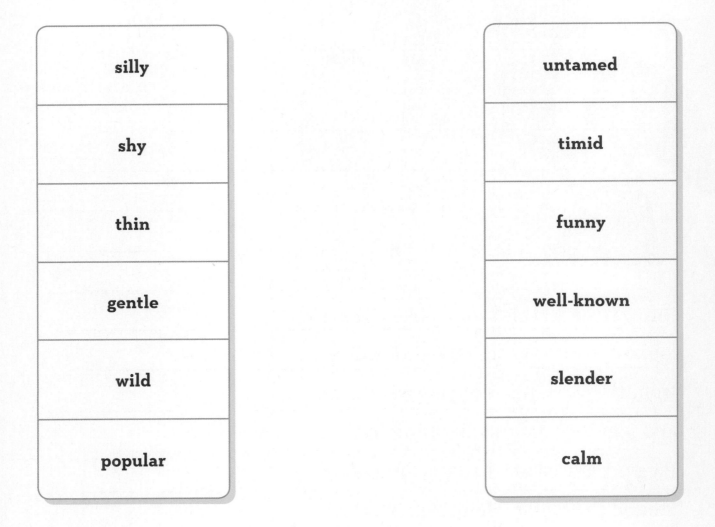

MAKE A DIFFERENCE!

Write about someone who has made a difference in your life.

_____

_____

_____

_____

_____

_____

_____

_____

_____

_____

_____

_____

_____

_____

CONNECT THE DOTS

Steve Irwin loved animals. He loved them so much, he started a zoo with his family. He also starred in a TV show about animals. Today, his kids have a TV show just like his.

Steve Irwin was known as

"The _____ Hunter."

Connect the dots to see the animal and then finish the sentence.

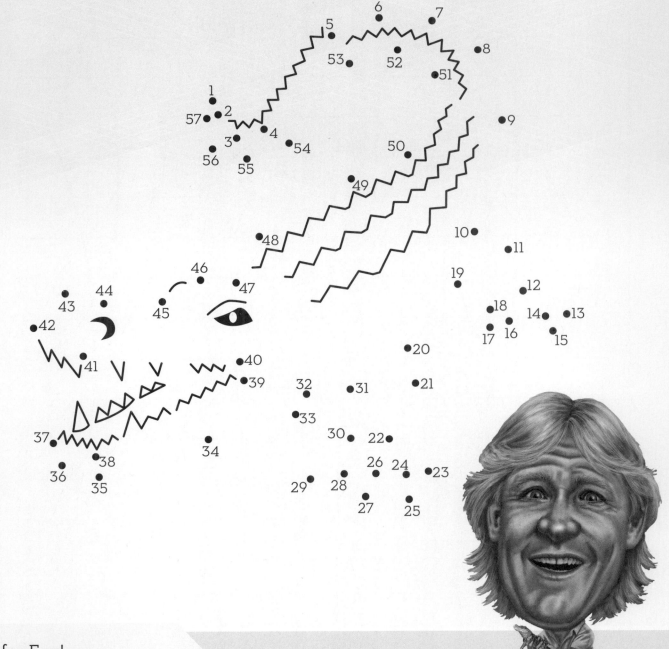

COLOR THE DOTS

Seabiscuit was a famous animal. What kind of animal was he?
Color the shapes that have a dot in them to discover the answer.

WHAT A MIX-UP!

Look at the picture and read the clue.
Unscramble the name of the famous Who Was? person.

Dr. Seuss

R D S S S E U

Clue: wrote books like *Green Eggs and Ham*

George Washington

E G O R G E   T O N I N G W A S H

Clue: first president of the United States

J. K. Rowling

K. J. L I N G R O W

Clue: wrote the Harry Potter books

Michelle Obama

M C H I E L L E   O A M A B

Clue: was first lady of the United States

King Tut

G N I K   U T T

Clue: was ruler of ancient Egypt

4

FAME!

Can you find the **bold-faced** words in the word search below?

F	A	M	O	U	S	F	Q	G	L	E	H
A	U	Z	X	R	E	G	E	N	D	H	I
Y	T	V	S	T	B	C	W	H	L	G	S
Q	H	I	N	V	E	N	T	O	R	M	T
F	O	K	Y	T	H	U	O	N	P	R	O
V	R	S	T	D	I	S	C	O	V	E	R
N	D	I	S	V	R	Z	H	R	N	O	Y
F	H	O	N	R	G	E	N	D	F	V	T
A	X	M	O	L	E	G	E	N	D	U	S
N	D	I	S	V	C	B	V	E	R	L	M

Author: person who writes a book

Discover: to find something new

Famous: well-known

Fan: someone who really likes a well-known person

History: the study of past events

Honor: to remember someone, showing great respect

Inventor: someone who made something new, like a machine

Legend: well-known person who did great things

5

ALL ABOUT WORDS

Complete the word box. For **Drawing**, draw a picture of someone creating something. For **Examples**, write examples of things that have been created, or made. For **Nonexamples**, write examples of things that haven't been created—things that occur naturally.

CREATE	
Definition in your own words	**Drawing**
to make	Pictures will vary.
Examples	**Nonexamples**
Answers will vary.	Answers will vary.

Synonym (word with the same meaning) ___ Answers will vary.

Antonym (word with the opposite meaning) ___ Answers will vary.

Related Words: Complete the word part to make a word with "create."

crea **tive**   **creat** ing   crea **tion**

8

DR. SEUSS RETELLING PYRAMID

author

What job did Dr. Seuss have?

The Lorax

What was Dr. Seuss's favorite book?

Answers will vary.

In three words, describe Dr. Seuss's books.

Answers will vary.

Besides his favorite, name another famous Dr. Seuss book.

What's the most interesting thing you learned about Dr. Seuss?

Answers will vary.

What else would you like to learn about Dr. Seuss?

Answers will vary.

9

TRUE OR FALSE?

Read each sentence about Maurice Sendak. Write **true** or **false** on the line. Then write another true sentence about Maurice Sendak on the last lines.

true 1. Maurice's father used to tell him scary stories.

false 2. Maurice's father was born in Italy.

false 3. Maurice didn't like scary stories.

true 4. *Where the Wild Things Are* was Maurice's most famous book.

false 5. The "Wild Things" in Maurice's book were robots from outer space.

true 6. Some people worried that Maurice's book was too scary for children.

7. **Answers will vary.**

12

FAMILY PORTRAIT

Pick a family member. Write a favorite memory.

_____
(title)

Answers will vary.

Write three words to describe this person.

13

PREFIX CONNECT

Helen Keller was one of the most famous people with **disabilities** in history. But she was **able** to read, write, and do so much more. The prefix **dis-** means "not" or the "opposite of." Draw a line to connect a prefix and a word to make a new word. Then write the new word above its definition.

dis = not or opposite of
re = again or back
mis = wrong, bad, or opposite

dis	write
re	read
dis	abled
re	appeared
mis	behaved

disabled
not able to do something, such as walk

rewrite
to write again

disappeared
no longer able to be seen

reread
to read again

misbehaved
acted in the wrong way

16

HAIKU

Haiku is a kind of poem. It has three lines. Each line has a specific number of syllables. Write a haiku describing Helen Keller.

Helen Keller

(5 syllables) ___ **Answers will vary.**
(7 syllables) ___
(5 syllables) ___

Now write a haiku describing you.

Me

(5 syllables) ___ **Answers will vary.**
(7 syllables) ___
(5 syllables) ___

haiku

17

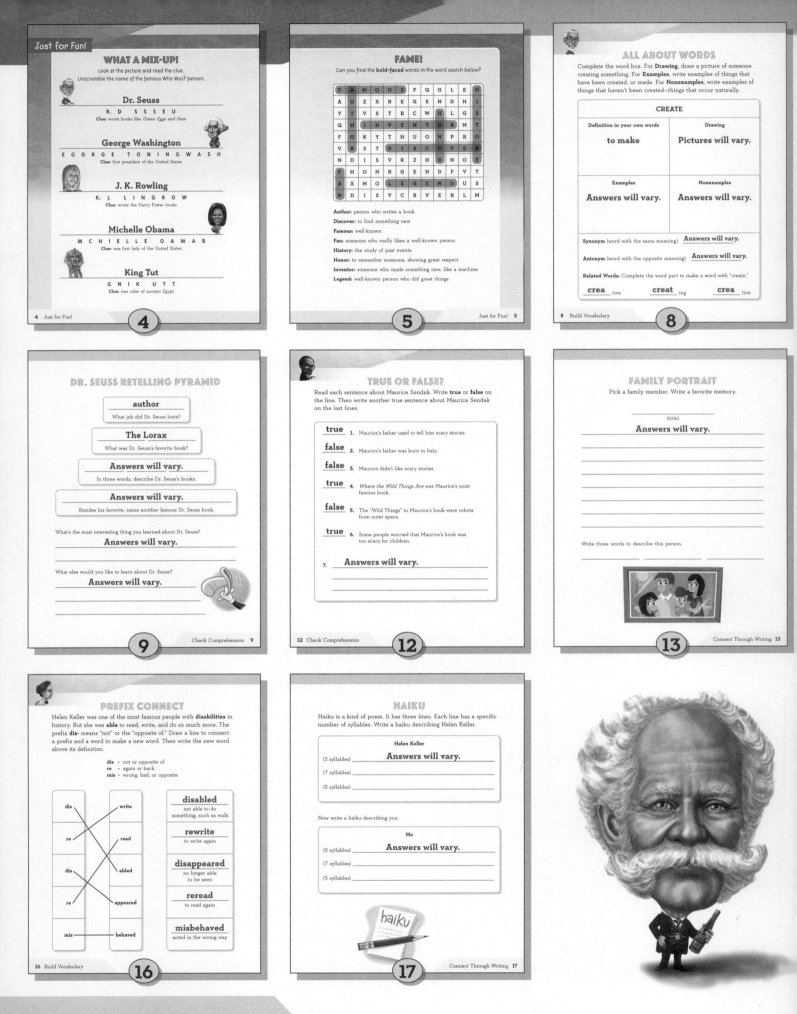

Just for Fun!

FAMOUS JOBS

Answer the clues to test what you know about these famous peoples' jobs.

CLUES

ACROSS
2. works to change things to help those who are treated badly
5. works for the government
7. writes books, stories, poems, and plays

DOWN
1. paints pictures
3. invents, or makes, new things
4. plays sports
6. appears in movies or plays

Laura Ingalls Wilder
Pablo Picasso
Steve Jobs
Charlie Chaplin

18 Just for Fun!

CROSSWORD

```
¹P A C T ²I V I S T
A     ³N
I     V
N     E     George
T     N     Washington
E     T
R     ⁴A
⁵P O L I T I C I ⁶A N
O     H     C
R     L     T
W R I T E R   O
      T     R
      E
```

Answer Choices

actor	politician
writer	athlete
inventor	painter
activist	

Jesse Owens
Jane Goodall

Just for Fun! 19

HIEROGLYPHS

The ancient Egyptians used symbols, called hieroglyphs, to write. Look at the hieroglyph key. Use it to write the words. Then draw a line from the word to its meaning.

Hieroglyph	Write Word	Meaning
	mummy	king or ruler
	pharaoh	a metal
	gold	a body preserved after death
	tomb	place where art and artifacts are kept
	museum	place someone is buried

22 Build Vocabulary

KING TUT RETELLING PYRAMID

Egypt
Where did Tut live?

Howard Carter
Who found Tut's tomb?

Answers will vary.
Name three things found in Tut's tomb.

Answers will vary.
Write a sentence about Tut.

What's the most interesting thing you learned about King Tut?
Answers will vary.

What else would you like to learn about King Tut?
Answers will vary.

Check Comprehension 23

SYNONYM BUCKETS

Synonyms are words that mean the same or nearly the same. Choose words from the word bank to fill the synonym buckets. Add other words you know.

Word Bank

bashful	wonderful	speaking	area
terrific	timid	community	chatting

neighborhood
area
community

shy
bashful
timid

great
wonderful
terrific

talking
speaking
chatting

26 Build Vocabulary

LETTER TIME

Kids wrote letters to Mister Rogers all the time. Write a letter to someone you know telling them about Mister Rogers.

Dear _____ ,
Answers will vary.

Your friend,
_____

Connect Through Writing 27

BLAST OFF!

Write four facts you learned about Sally Ride.

1. **Answers will vary.**
2.
3.
4.

30 Check Comprehension

Answer Key **91**

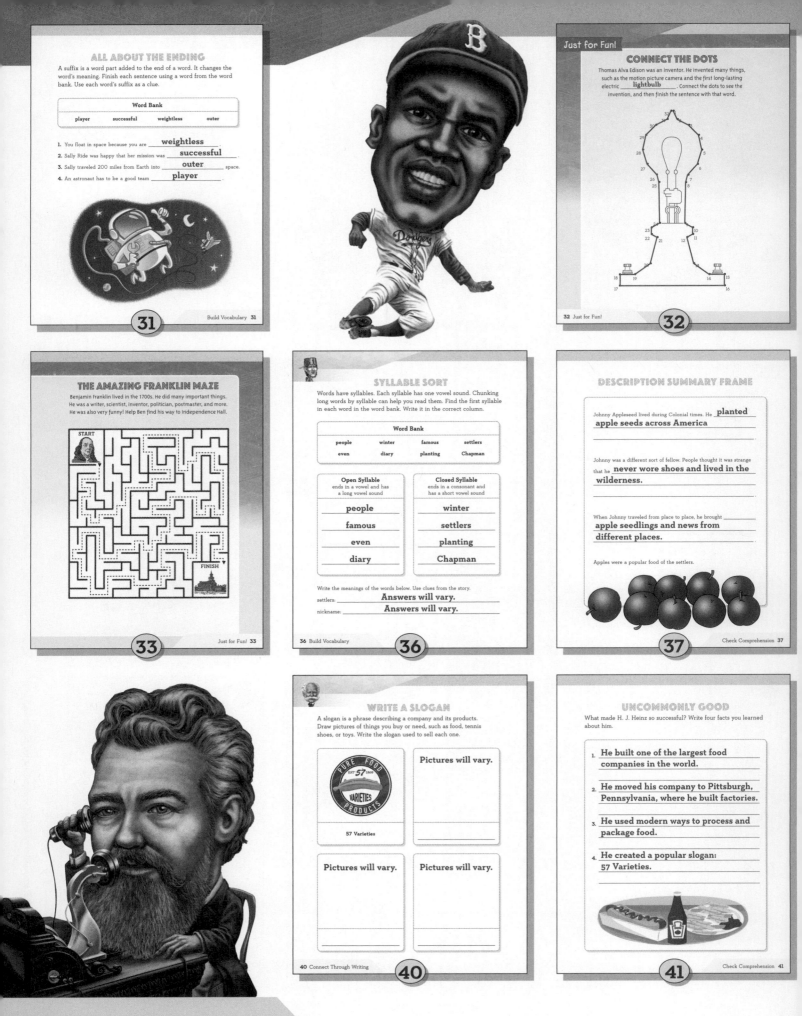

ALL ABOUT THE ENDING

A suffix is a word part added to the end of a word. It changes the word's meaning. Finish each sentence using a word from the word bank. Use each word's suffix as a clue.

Word Bank			
player	successful	weightless	outer

1. You float in space because you are **weightless**
2. Sally Ride was happy that her mission was **successful**
3. Sally traveled 200 miles from Earth into **outer** space.
4. An astronaut has to be a good team **player**

31   Build Vocabulary 31

CONNECT THE DOTS

Thomas Alva Edison was an inventor. He invented many things, such as the motion picture camera and the first long-lasting electric **lightbulb**. Connect the dots to see the invention, and then finish the sentence with that word.

32 Just for Fun!   32

THE AMAZING FRANKLIN MAZE

Benjamin Franklin lived in the 1700s. He did many important things. He was a writer, scientist, inventor, politician, postmaster, and more. He was also very funny! Help Ben find his way to Independence Hall.

START
FINISH

33   Just for Fun! 33

SYLLABLE SORT

Words have syllables. Each syllable has one vowel sound. Chunking long words by syllable can help you read them. Find the first syllable in each word in the word bank. Write it in the correct column.

Word Bank			
people	winter	famous	settlers
even	diary	planting	Chapman

Open Syllable ends in a vowel and has a long vowel sound	Closed Syllable ends in a consonant and has a short vowel sound
people	winter
famous	settlers
even	planting
diary	Chapman

Write the meanings of the words below. Use clues from the story.

settlers: **Answers will vary.**
nickname: **Answers will vary.**

36 Build Vocabulary   36

DESCRIPTION SUMMARY FRAME

Johnny Appleseed lived during Colonial times. He **planted apple seeds across America**

Johnny was a different sort of fellow. People thought it was strange that he **never wore shoes and lived in the wilderness.**

When Johnny traveled from place to place, he brought **apple seedlings and news from different places.**

Apples were a popular food of the settlers.

37   Check Comprehension 37

WRITE A SLOGAN

A slogan is a phrase describing a company and its products. Draw pictures of things you buy or need, such as food, tennis shoes, or toys. Write the slogan used to sell each one.

PURE FOOD / EST 57 1869 / VARIETIES / PRODUCTS

57 Varieties

Pictures will vary.

Pictures will vary.

Pictures will vary.

40 Connect Through Writing   40

UNCOMMONLY GOOD

What made H. J. Heinz so successful? Write four facts you learned about him.

1. He built one of the largest food companies in the world.
2. He moved his company to Pittsburgh, Pennsylvania, where he built factories.
3. He used modern ways to process and package food.
4. He created a popular slogan: 57 Varieties.

41   Check Comprehension 41

OUR FIRST FLAG

Color the flag using details from the story.

Write three interesting facts about the flag.

1. It was based on a sketch by George Ross, Robert Morris, and George Washington.
2. It had 13 red and white stripes. It also had a blue square with 13 stars.
3. Some people think it was sewn by Betsy Ross.

YOU'RE A LEGEND!

Write about someone who is, or could become, a legend because of their great deeds.

Answers will vary.

Just for Fun!

COMIC TIME!

Make your own comic strip. Tell the story of someone famous. Or tell about a big event in your life.

Pictures will vary.

PROBLEM/SOLUTION SUMMARY FRAME

George Washington Carver was a scientist and an inventor. He spent his life solving problems.

One problem he solved had to do with the use of peanuts. Peanuts were a problem because **farmers couldn't make much money growing them.**

Carver solved this problem by **showing farmers how to grow them to add nutrients to the soil** and **creating a booklet showing all the things that could be made from peanuts.**

Now we use peanuts for many things. Farmers make a lot of money growing them, too.

YUM! IT'S RECIPE TIME!

What food do you like made from peanuts? Fill in the recipe card for this food. Or make up your own recipe!

Recipe   Peanut _____

Ingredients:

1. _____ **Answers will vary.**
2. _____
3. _____
4. _____

BROTHER AND SISTER WORDS

Some words are related, like brothers and sisters. They come from the same base word. Look at the words in the word bank. Use them to fill in the chart.

Word Bank			
perform	magic	excite	dance
performer	magical	excited	dancer
performance	magician	excitement	dancing

NOUN names a person, place, or thing	VERB action word	ADJECTIVE describing word
performance	perform	magical
performer	excite	excited
magic	dance	
magician	dancing	
excitement		
dancer		

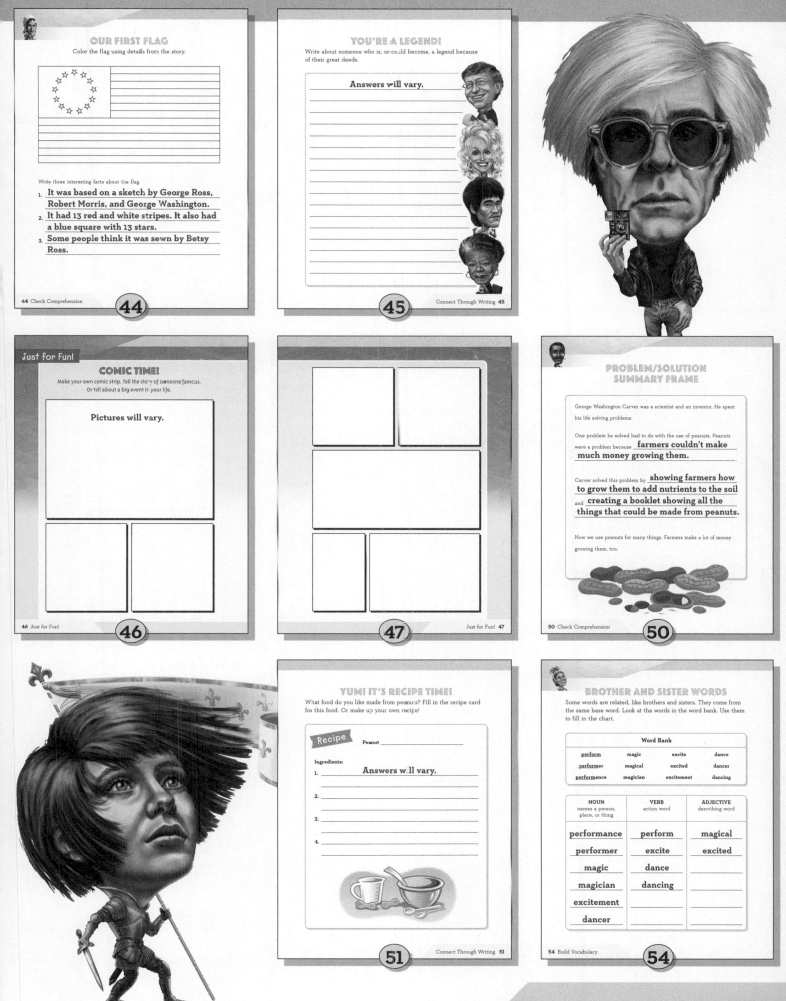

ALL ABOUT MARIA

Fill in each blank to show what you learned about Maria Tallchief.

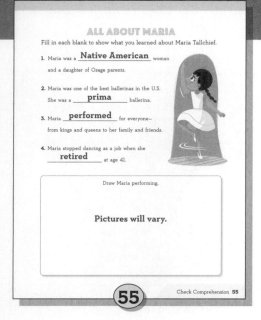

1. Maria was a **Native American** woman and a daughter of Osage parents.

2. Maria was one of the best ballerinas in the U.S. She was a **prima** ballerina.

3. Maria **performed** for everyone— from kings and queens to her family and friends.

4. Maria stopped dancing as a job when she **retired** at age 41.

Draw Maria performing.

Pictures will vary.

ALL ABOUT WORDS

Look at the word in each soccer ball. Write a fact from the story using each word.

poor — Pelé grew up in a poor neighborhood in Brazil.

advantage — Pelé had one advantage. His father was a great soccer player and could teach him how to play well.

league — There were few soccer leagues for kids when Pelé was young.

positions — There are many positions soccer players play on the field.

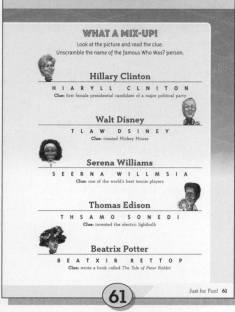

WHAT A MIX-UP!

Look at the picture and read the clue. Unscramble the name of the famous Who Was? person.

Hillary Clinton

H I A R Y L L   C L N I T O N

Clue: first female presidential candidate of a major political party

Walt Disney

T L A W   D S I N E Y

Clue: created Mickey Mouse

Serena Williams

S E E R N A   W I L L M S I A

Clue: one of the world's best tennis players

Thomas Edison

T H S A M O   S O N E D I

Clue: invented the electric lightbulb

Beatrix Potter

B E A T X I R   R E T T O P

Clue: wrote a book called *The Tale of Peter Rabbit*

GAME TIME!

Write about a game or sport you know how to play.

Keys to Playing

1.   **Answers will vary.**
2.
3.
4.

Picture of Kids Playing _____

Pictures will vary.

Why I Recommend It

Answers will vary.

READING BRAILLE

Look at the braille chart. Write words from the story using the chart. Draw a line from the word to its meaning.

Braille	Write Word	Meaning
	blind	system of writing using dots
	invent	not able to see
	braille	to make something new
	terrible	very bad

SEARCH FOR IT!

Read the facts about some well-known people. Find the **bold-faced** words in the word search.

C	M	A	G	I	C	I	A	N	L	D	Y
M	O	V	S	C	O	O	D	X	B	L	V
R	V	P	A	D	O	X	T	O	N	S	M
U	I	T	V	Y	K	D	L	C	S	I	U
A	E	X	P	E	D	I	T	I	O	N	I
M	S	A	T	E	C	H	O	D	L	G	N
U	M	L	E	D	Y	T	R	W	Q	E	P
S	Z	X	S	L	A	D	Y	U	I	R	F
I	J	M	S	H	C	O	L	O	P	T	U
C	H	O	C	O	L	A	T	E	R	R	M

Dolly Parton is a famous **singer**.
Julia Child taught people how to **cook**.
Harry Houdini was a master **magician**.
Bruce Lee was a martial artist who made **movies**.
Elvis Presley was known as "The King of Rock 'n' Roll" **music**.
Milton Hershey was a candymaker, famous for his **chocolate**.
Eleanor Roosevelt was once the first **lady** of the U.S.
Sacagawea helped Lewis and Clark on their **expedition**.

SEQUENCE SUMMARY FRAME

When Louis Braille was three years old, **he had a terrible accident that left him blind.**

At age 10, **he went to Paris to study at a school for the blind.**

There, he **learned to read and learned about "night writing."**

Finally, at age 15, **he invented his own system of reading for the blind, called braille.**

Today, people all over the world still use braille.

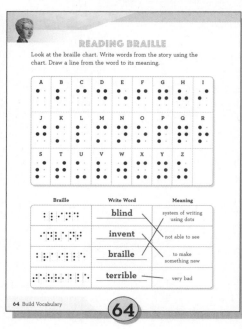

---

94 Answer Key

ALL ABOUT WORDS

Complete the word box. For **Drawing**, draw a picture that shows someone protecting something. For **Examples**, write examples of things that are protected. For **Nonexamples** write examples of things that are not protected.

PROTECT	
Definition in your own words	Drawing
to keep safe	Pictures will vary.
Examples	Nonexamples
Answers will vary.	Answers will vary.

Synonym (word with the same meaning) ____ guard

Antonym (word with the opposite meaning) ____ endanger

Related Words: Complete the word part to make a word with "protect."

protec ___ tion   protect ___ ing   protec ___ tive

68 Build Vocabulary

68

FASCINATING FACTS

Write four facts you learned from the story about Michelle Obama.

1. Family always came first for Michelle Obama.

2. Michelle met Barack Obama when she was a lawyer.

3. She was the first African American first lady.

4. Michelle had rules for her daughters to follow.

Check Comprehension 69

69

SONIA SUMMARY

Write a summary of "Nothing Could Stop Her." Use four sentences. Include only the most important facts.

Answers will vary.

72 Check Comprehension

72

WHEN I WAS A KID

Sonia's visit to the doctor changed her life. Write about a memory from your life—happy or sad. Why was it an important day or event?

Answers will vary.

Connect Through Writing 73

73

Just for Fun!

FAMOUS PEOPLE

Answer the clues to test what you know about these famous people.

CLUES

ACROSS

2. Rosa Parks was called the "First Lady of Civil ____ Rights .

3. Frida Kahlo was a painter living in ____ Mexico .

4. Neil Armstrong was the first person to step on the ____ moon .

6. Roberto Clemente was a great ____ baseball player.

DOWN

1. Amelia Earhart flew across the Atlantic ____ Ocean .

2. Harriet Tubman led enslaved people to freedom on the Underground ____ Railroad .

5. Anne Frank wrote a famous ____ diary .

Frida Kahlo

Rosa Parks

Neil Armstrong

74 Just for Fun!

74

CROSSWORD

Roberto Clemente

Harriet Tubman

```
 ¹O   ²R I G H T S
  C   A
 ³M E X I C O
  E   I
  A   L
 ⁴M O O N  R    ⁷D
       O    I
  Answer Choices
   diary     ⁶B A S E B A L L
   Rights         R
   moon           Y
   Railroad
   baseball
   Ocean
   Mexico
```

Anne Frank

Amelia Earhart

Just for Fun! 75

75

WHAT IS A FAIRY TALE?

Use facts from the story. Write what you know about fairy tales.

Characteristics

1. It is a quest story where someone is looking for something.

2. It is usually about a hero who overcomes evil.

3. It usually has magic.

4. It often has make-believe creatures, like giants or elves.

Examples

1. Answers will vary.

2. _____

3. _____

4. _____

78 Check Comprehension

78

FAIRY TALE RETELLING

Choose your favorite fairy tale. Write a retelling. Or write your own funny version of the tale.

> Answers will vary.

79

DEFINE, EXAMPLE, ASK

Look at each word. Write a definition for the word. Use clues from the story. Then write an example sentence using the word. Finally, write a question using the word that you could ask a friend.

horrified	Define:	**shocked and scared**
	Example:	**Answers will vary.**
	Ask:	
improve	Define:	**make better**
	Example:	**Answers will vary.**
	Ask:	
declared	Define:	**stated; said with confidence**
	Example:	**Answers will vary.**
	Ask:	
diplomat	Define:	**person who works for the government**
	Example:	**Answers will vary.**
	Ask:	

82

MALALA RETELLING PYRAMID

Malala
What is the girl's name?

United Nations
What organization made July 12, 2013, Malala Day?

Answers will vary.
In three words, describe Malala.

Finish this sentence: Malala wanted **to make sure all girls could go to school.**

What's the most interesting thing you learned about Malala?
Answers will vary.

What else would you like to learn about Malala?
Answers will vary.

83

SYNONYM MATCH

Synonyms are words that mean the same or almost the same. Match the synonyms.

silly	untamed
shy	timid
thin	funny
gentle	well-known
wild	slender
popular	calm

Write a synonym for each word below.

quiet **Answers will vary.**   fast **Answers will vary.**

86

MAKE A DIFFERENCE!

Write about someone who has made a difference in your life.

> **Answers will vary.**

87

Just for Fun!

CONNECT THE DOTS

Steve Irwin loved animals. He loved them so much, he started a zoo with his family. He also starred in a TV show about animals. Today, his kids have a TV show just like his.

Steve Irwin was known as

"The **Crocodile** Hunter."

Connect the dots to see the animal and then finish the sentence.

88

COLOR THE DOTS

Seabiscuit was a famous animal. What kind of animal was he? Color the shapes that have a dot in them to discover the answer.

89

---

96 Answer Key